Mommy,
Where are you?

By Tera F. Howard, MD

Illustrated by Addy McNew, M.Ed.

AuthorHouse™
1663 Liberty Drive
Bloomington, IN 47403
www.authorhouse.com
Phone: 1 (800) 839-8640

Published by AuthorHouse 04/11/2017

ISBN: 978-1-5246-7102-0 (sc)
978-1-5246-7104-4 (hc)
978-1-5246-7103-7 (e)

Library of Congress Control Number: 2017901737

Print information available on the last page.

authorHOUSE®

To working mommies
(and their children) everywhere ...

Mommy, it's morning time. Where are you?

1

I am helping sick people get well.

Mommy, it's breakfast time. Where are you?

3

Mommy, it's school time.
Where are you?

5

I am bringing justice to all.

6

Mommy, it's lunchtime. Where are you?

I am feeding the hungry.

8

I am fighting for our freedom.

10

Mommy, it's homework time. Where are you?

I am helping others learn.

12

Mommy, it's playtime. Where are you?

I am bringing people home safely.

Mommy, it's bedtime. Where are you?

I am telling others about the
world around them.

18

Mommy, I need you. Where are you?

I am right here.

My Darling,

I'll hold you close,

And won't let go,

But when I'm gone,

Please always know,

I'm in your heart,

And you, in mine,

For all of time.

Love, Mommy

Author Tera Frederick Howard is a wife, mother and physician. She completed her undergraduate degree at Wake Forest University, her medical and public health degrees at Vanderbilt University, and her residency in obstetrics and gynecology at Northwestern University. She currently practices general obstetrics and gynecology in Birmingham, Al. She is the wife of Thomas N. Howard and mother of Nayla Ann-Marie Howard, who serves as the primary inspiration for her books.

Illustrator Adrienne Hatcher Mcnew works as a high school counselor for Metro Nashville Public Schools. She attended the College of Charleston for her undergraduate training and received her Master of Education with a concentration in Secondary School Counseling from the Citadel in Charleston, SC. She currently resides in Nashville, TN with her husband Matt. Tera and Adrienne met at Sumter High School in Sumter, SC and have been friends since.

Printed in the United States
By Bookmasters